Alex Eats the Rainbow

A Book about Healthy Eating

by Kerry Dinmont

Published by The Child's World®
1980 Lookout Drive • Mankato, MN 56003-1705
800-599-READ • www.childsworld.com

ISBN 9781503820203
LCCN 2016960941

Printed in the United States of America
PA02340

Alex eats a food rainbow today.

What **fruits** and **vegetables** does Alex eat?

Alex eats oatmeal for breakfast. He puts red strawberries on top.

Alex eats orange carrots
for a snack.

Alex packs a lunch. He adds a yellow banana.

Lettuce and cucumbers are green vegetables. Alex puts them on his sandwich.

Alex snacks on blueberries before supper.

Alex eats purple beets with supper.

Alex has eaten many colorful foods today. Fruits and vegetables keep his body healthy and strong.

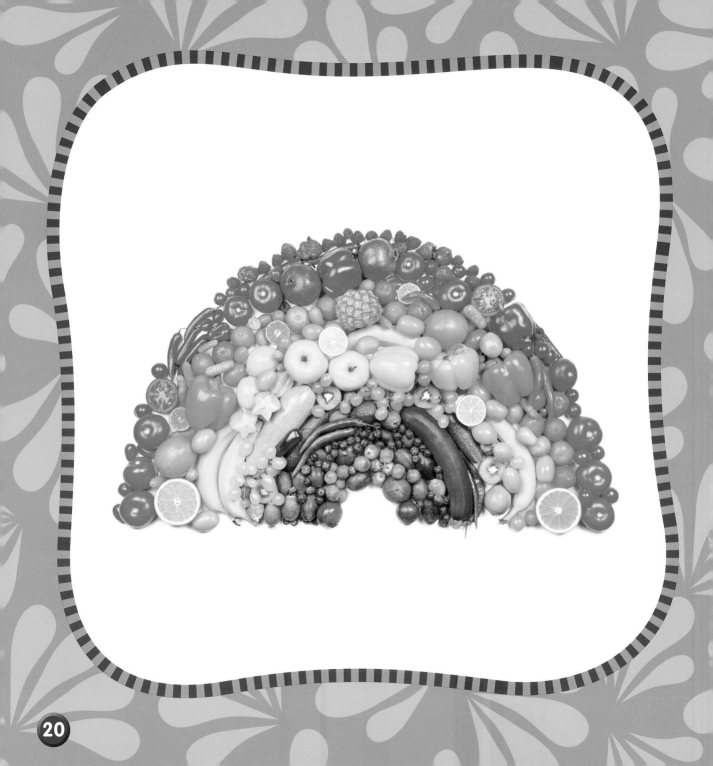

What colors of the rainbow have you eaten today?

fruits (FROOTS) Fruits are the parts of plants that have seeds. Fruits are often sweet and can be eaten.

vegetables (VEJ-tuh-buhlz) Vegetables are parts of plants that can be eaten. Lettuce and cucumbers are vegetables.

Extended Learning Activities

1. What color is each food that Alex eats?

2. Think of the foods you have eaten. What colors were they?

3. Look at the photos in this book. How do they help you understand the text?

To Learn More

Books

Butterworth, Chris. *How Did That Get in My Lunchbox?*
Sommerville, MA: Candlewick Press, 2011.

Harris, Robie H. *What's So Yummy?*
Somerville, MA: Candlewick Press, 2014.

Web Sites

Visit our Web site for links about healthy eating:
childsworld.com/links

Note to Parents, Teachers, and Librarians: We routinely verify our Web links to make sure
they are safe and active sites. So encourage your readers to check them out!

About the Author

Kerry Dinmont is a children's book author who enjoys art and nature. She lives in Montana with her two Norwegian elkhounds.